That's Us

Written by Jo Windsor

Some animals stay together
in groups.

These fish swim together
to keep safe.
A group of fish
is called a school.

These birds stay together
to keep safe, too.
A group of birds
is called a flock.

These penguins stay together
on the ice.
A group of penguins
is called a colony.

The penguins stay together in a group to keep warm.

These elephants stay together
in a group.
A group of elephants
is called a herd.

When a baby elephant is born,
some of the elephants
help it to stand up.

These meerkats are
in a group, too.

Some of the big meerkats
look after the little meerkats.
They *babysit* the little meerkats
so other meerkats can eat.

The lions stay together
to hunt for food.
A group of lions
is called a pride.

The wolves stay together
to hunt for food, too.
A group of wolves
is called a pack.

Some animals stay together
in groups to keep safe or warm.
Some animals stay together
to help or to hunt.

14

Index

▬▬ Guide Notes

Title: That's Us
Stage: Early (3) – Blue

Genre: Non-fiction
Approach: Guided Reading
Processes: Thinking Critically, Exploring Language, Processing Information
Visual Focus: Photographs (static images), Index
Word Count: 172

THINKING CRITICALLY
(sample questions)
- What do you think this book is going to tell us?
- What groups of animals can you see on the front cover?
- Focus the children's attention on the index. Ask: "What animals are you going to find out about in this book?"
- If you want to find out about penguins, what page would you look on?
- If you want to find out about elephants, what page would you look on?
- Look at pages 2 and 3. Why do you think these animals are staying together?
- Look at pages 12 and 13. Why do you think these animals are in groups?
- Look at page 14. Why do some animals stay together in groups?

EXPLORING LANGUAGE

Terminology
Title, cover, photographs, author, photographers

Vocabulary
Interest words: groups, flock, colony, herd, pride, pack
High-frequency words: other, these, when, so, eat
Positional words: in, on, up
Compound word: babysit

Print Conventions
Capital letter for sentence beginnings, full stops, commas